SMALL IS UGLY

SMALL IS UGLY

LAB CHAUDHURI

PARTRIDGE

To order additional copies of this book, contact
Partridge India
000 800 10062 62
orders.india@partridgepublishing.com

www.partridgepublishing.com/india

CONTENTS

To my wife Krishna and my son Ayan

FOREWORD

I had not planned to write a foreword to my father's book initially for two reasons. Firstly, I wanted to publish this book in the purest form as possible, exactly as my father had written it and secondly because I felt intimated by the prospect of having to write a foreword for a book written by Lab Chaudhuri, an acknowledged expert of his time in the area of Small Scale Industries and a copiously published business columnist. He is the most brilliant human being I have ever known and is someone who I have been in awe of throughout my life. It was my wife Kamalika who insisted that I write a foreword so that the reader can get to know a little bit more about him, rather than me simply publishing whatever he had written.

Since he had expired in 1993, more than 22 years back, it would be impossible to look him up on Facebook or LinkedIn and hence it is not really out of place that I write something so that the reader gets to know something about him.

Lab Chaudhuri was born in Kolkata to a well-educated, upper-middle class family (I take the liberty of using the word "upper" since my grandfather was a renowned Barrister of Calcutta High Court). Baba excelled in studies and was a topper throughout. He obtained a double–promotion from his Alma Mater (Calcutta Boys' School) and was a rank-holder in Calcutta University in B.Com, graduating from St. Xavier's College, Calcutta. He was a Masters degree holder from Calcutta University and trained as a Management Accountant from the Institute of Cost and Management Accountants, London. After completing University, he joined State Bank of India, the largest bank in the country, as a Probationary Officer.

It was in one of his postings that he became very interested in the area of Small Scale Industries. At heart, Baba had always been an academic and not a mere paper-pusher. Hence he was never content with progressing his career by staying on and merely doing his job well (which he already was). He had always wanted to learn more about areas that deeply interested him and so he decided to move on so that he could explore the particular area of Small Scale Industries. An explorer cannot come to know everything about an unknown place merely by reading a book written by someone else about it – he necessarily has to step out of his living room and take great pains to actually visit the place to understand its people and culture. Similarly, my father realized that the only way to really understand this sector was to actually go and work in it. Eventually, he resigned from his job in State Bank of India (quite an unthinkable decision back in the early 1980s) and joined a small scale firm. Subsequently he worked in a few others as well in the various stages of the life-cycle of a firm. This book is a culmination of his experiences at these various small-scale firms.

Endowed with both kinds of intelligence by modern definition (Academic and Emotional), he was not merely successful in academics and work but was also well loved by everyone whose life he touched - his family, friends, colleagues and workers. Witty and helpful would be the terms I would use to describe his personality. Ever helpful, he would take great pains to assist others in their times of need, sometimes at the cost of his own convenience. I happened to attend the same school he did and my identity amongst most of the teaching and non-teaching staff in the school was simply (not without a twinge of jealousy back then, I must finally admit!) Lab Chaudhuri's son. And all this was years after he had graduated. He had more friends and well-wishers than I can recount. Even after 22 years of his demise, he is still fondly remembered in various circles.

It feels very unfair that such a brilliant and likeable human being would be afflicted with a devastating and degenerative disease in the prime of his life, which subsequently resulted in his early demise at the age of 44. However, it is pointless questioning God's judgment on these issues. All I know is that the last few years of his life progressively became difficult – not only did he have to stop working but slowly became unable to write and finally even unable to hold up a book on his own to read - essentially stopped being able to do things which were so important to him.

Afflicted with such a crippling condition, it is very easy for a human being to give up on life and live out the remaining days morose and dejected - and one cannot blame him or her for this. But I never saw the slightest hint of defeat or dejection in him – in fact, he continued to write articles and publish them in the leading newspapers of his time such as The Telegraph, The Statesman, Business Standard and the like. Because he could not write by himself owing to the onset of his disease, he hired the services of a typist to whom he dictated his articles. He always believed he would recover, despite all the doctors having told him otherwise to his face.

We often hear about stories of courage in the face of adversities, where a human being has to overcome a number of odds to achieve some goal or end. Though it has been painful to witness his suffering during the last few years of his life, I consider myself to be extremely lucky to have witnessed this resilience and fortitude in my father, in the face of so much adversity and these lessons in facing the vicissitudes of life have been invaluable. I would say that the only thing he had going for him during those trying times was a wife who was intensely devoted to him. He may be long deceased but his courage and spirit continue to inspire me and indeed my entire family. I hope that my daughter Nayantrika, for her own sake, is able to draw as much inspiration from her grandfather as I have. Baba had written this book during his final years and departed for his heavenly abode before getting it published. I chanced upon the manuscript a couple of years back while going through some his old files. Publishing this book is but a small tribute to him.

Ayan Chaudhuri

Son of Lab Chaudhuri

Singapore, September 2015

ABOUT THE AUTHOR

The author (deceased) served for eight years as an Officer in a leading Nationalized Bank of this Country, mostly in the small Loans Department at its Head Office. Resigning from the  Bank's services, he served as a Financial Controller in succession in three small scale industries, one healthy, one sick and the other "rehabilitated". Therefore, he has first hand experience, on both sides of the table, so to say, of what he is writing about. Subsequently, he was engaged in consultancy work, mainly giving advice to the small sector on how to run the units successfully.

CHAPTER 1

INTRODUCTION

It is first necessary to define the persons about whom this book is written. I have used the term "Small men" or "Small businessmen" rather generously in the following chapters and it would be in order if these terms are put in their proper perspectives right at the beginning.

I have purposely not used the term "Small scale Industry", as it has a definite definition (Value of machinery not exceeding 20 lacs). Whereas the small businessman does come under the purview of small scale industry, it is not my intention to include all small scale industries in my definition of the small businessmen. This book is directed to the vast majority of persons who are eager to become industrialists without unfortunately any capital backing. This mass of humanity, only peculiar to this nation, with dreams in their heart are fed by constant Government propaganda of easy availability of capital from the many government owned financial institutions. Therefore they take heart to launch upon a business venture with their brains and brawns and their life's dream as their only investment - only to come to grief when they realize later on that they had been fed on false promises. It is about these men that this book is written.

My experience with small industries in general has led me to believe that small industries, without a sound capital base, have no future in this country. It is the fundamental principle of any business that there should be a proper and healthy capital base. Years of experimentation to the contrary have proved the Indians Pundits wrong. The Government or India, in an effort to bolster the employment potential on a small investment, has given encouragement to the small man to set up an industry of his own. The propaganda machine worked overtime spreading the message that lack of capital resources was no bar in starting a business venture, as there were a number of liberalized schemes of the government owned financial institutions to ensure quick and easy availability of the same. The entrepreneurial class, gullible as it is, was taken in by this promise and at times hastily conceived industrial units were set up. This led to temporary alleviation of the nation's difficulty - in the form of employment and industrial production - but greater hazards were to follow.

The reliance on the human factor for the success of small industries is so high as to render them not viable from the start. Undue emphasis has to be placed on the kindness of others - the government, the financial institutions, the business community and the public at large - for the small units to ultimately survive. Each case is unique, and the modalities of dealing with the small industries cannot ever be formalized. Each has to be dealt with separately and no proper guideline, except in broad general terms, can be laid down. This adds to the confusion in so far as the government agencies and financial institutions specifically charged with helping the small men are concerned as proper orientation of the personnel is necessary. Not only should they be well-versed with the rule book, but they should be able to temper justice with mercy. In view of this requirement, assistance to small industries has been unsatisfactory as it is foolish to expect the same standard of conduct from all the employees of the aforesaid agencies or institutions.

Small industries by their basic construction and structure are doomed to ultimate decay. On the one hand their fortunes are inextricably linked with the personalities of one or two men (a detailed discussion on this aspect in a subsequent chapter), but also they cannot run conforming to sound business principles. With low capitalization, low profitability, tendencies of overtrading, precarious liquidity position, etc., it can hardly be expected to run on sound principles. And what is worse the small industries cannot but run flouting these sound principles for it is a question of do or perish, the word "do" connoting keeping one's head above the water by all means.

Because of this inalienable feature of small industries, forward planning is necessarily absent. So also is the necessity of updating technology, which suffers in the hands of small men. Because the small industries are personality-oriented, knowledgeableness about the production process is as far as the entrepreneur would allow himself to be up-to-date with. Then again because of chronic shortage of capital and easy availability of cheap labour, these small industries are tempted to make unavoidable compromises, which are only poor substitutes of what in reality could have been done.

The following articles are devoted exclusively to the problem faced by small industries. I have purposely not taken resort to the third worst kind of lies, i.e. statistics because I believe that the problems of the small sector have not been looked upon in the proper perspective. And unless the government addresses itself urgently to these specific ills while posing to help the small men, the whole culture of small business is bound to crumble sooner or later. Encouragement of the small, admittedly beneficial in many ways, is bound to suffer a serious setback if the government fails to turn its attention on their basic drawbacks and it is primarily for this purpose that this book is written.

I have been, for the last three years, occasionally writing in The Telegraph and The Statesman of Calcutta about the problems of small business. Most of the following chapters are verbatim as well as edited copies of articles which have appeared in these newspapers from time to time.

The choice before the powers that be are clear – to let go things as they are being done, with the consequent extinction of the small business or taking the bull by the horn and render positive help to this class of small businessmen, so that it is able to survive and flourish. What needs to be emphasized is that deeds must match the words and pronouncements about the need to encourage the small sector must be accompanied with proper support.

CHAPTER 2

STATE OF AFFAIRS TODAY

In the present day the financial institutions in pursuance of the government industrial policy have increased considerably their portfolio of advances to the small sector. But one must pause to consider the ultimate price of this generosity. The business of financial institutions has recorded a high spurt in activity owing to large scale advances to the small sector. But it has to be understood that there exists a total lack of infrastructure for proper house-keeping and follow-up of the advances made. And the small man very often withers away for lack of proper guidance and counseling which the bankers are by the terms of the industrial policy expected to do, but they cannot owing to lack of proper facilities in the form of properly trained and attuned manpower.

That the small man is basically a helpless creature who is not appreciated by anyone and decisions on financing matters usually follow the same yard-sticks as are applicable in the case of his big brethren. Such is the case because of improper understanding of the peculiarities of the small ventures. It has to be remembered that unlike the established and financially strong business houses, the small men entering into business ventures cannot withstand the slightest adversity and are likely to buckle under pressure of any kind, however slight it may be. This is principally because of lack of monetary resources at their disposal. Not only is the small man sensitive to fund shortage, but his survival is dependent upon the smooth and timely availability of other inputs.

This is exactly where much needed governmental intervention is required if this sector is to be nurtured. Today, almost in every field, the small units are left to themselves to govern the affairs without much assistance regarding ensuring smooth availability of the inputs of production. Although it is true that there have been attempts from time to time to assure the small units regarding supply of various production inputs, in reality they are left to the same uncertain market forces as are their big brothers. And as has been stated earlier, unable to withstand the slightest adversity, death/decay is the ultimate result.

In the presence of the above state of affairs it is indeed a hard struggle for small units to cut a niche for themselves and strike roots in this country. Added to all this is the peculiarity of the small business man in that the personal character of the owner is firmly and inalienably attached to the business venture he runs. There· is no conscious effort on the part of the entrepreneurs to dissociate himself from the firm he runs. Therefore the personality and character of the firm becomes inextricably that of the owners and sooner or later a personality cult develops in business dealings. The enterprise without the proprietor cannot stand on its two legs. Hence with incapacitation or death of the owner, the business ventures are more likely than ever, to also come to an abrupt halt owing primarily to lack of continuity.

The difference between the small industries and the big ones is that in an age of standardization and impersonal business dealings, the former brings a touch of personal warmth to all business relationships. The equivalent service of "made to measure" in the tailoring trade is offered by the small man. And this service is much sought after by the various customers as it ensures personal attention to his needs. Therefore the small industry takes a personal character - one which is tied to that of the proprietor. This hinders development of the small businessman from acquiring the characteristics of a big one and ultimately become detrimental to smooth succession.

Added to this state of fragility is the tendency of all financial institutions to look up on the small business men as an unscrupulous lot who is bent upon plundering public money. Such an attitude, borne out of inadequate appreciation of the small man's problems and wrong motivational attitude of the concerned personnel, is indeed inimical to the proliferation and prosperity of this sector of the economy. In the process what the financial institutions do not understand is that they themselves are perhaps responsible for the entrepreneur's change of attitude.

The financial institutions have complete sway over the firm's behavioral patterns because the small man is completely dependent upon them for the provision of this important input - money. Therefore the small man is tyrannized by the personnel of the financial institutions, and is led to conform to certain activities which run counter to the business activity of the small unit. A simple example would suffice to illustrate this phenomenon. The practice of fixing margins in borrowing accounts of the assisted units is an accepted thing in the banking circle. Although much lip service is paid to such concepts as "need based financing" such are given the convenient go-by at the time of fixation of borrowing limit. It is insisted upon that the borrower, if he has to enjoy borrowing facilities, has to bring in matching margins (20-25% normally). Such an obstinate demand is made irrespective of the borrowers' ability to raise and invest the required margin money. In his anxiety to get things started he would perhaps resort to deliberate "mistruth" as over-invoicing arrangement with machinery suppliers and falsification of the stock statement.

What is being sought to be suggested is that the financial institutions can play a prominent role in seeing to it that the small borrowers follow a straight and narrow path of probity and honour if only their difficulties are properly appreciated. Self-less appreciation of the small man's peculiar difficulty is the crying need of the hour – but can hardly be expected in the context of diverse personnel manning widely proliferated front line branch units of the financial institutions.

It is no surprise, therefore, that with the declaration by the government, so prominently advertised, that the financial institutions are virtually inundated by applications for grant of finance to the small industrial sector. It has also to be appreciated that the financial institutions cannot do justice to each and every applicant because of lack of infrastructural facilities, especially trained and motivated manpower. In the process internal house-keeping in the form of servicing existing accounts, does take a toll.

In the matter of making advances, some amount of subjectivity is inescapable. It would be helpful for the economy if that subjectivity errs on the side of liberalization rather than on stinginess. For, it is a fact that most small units die a natural death owing to lack of adequate and timely capital.

To streamline the entire process of helping the small man to set up a business venture, it is indeed important for us to minimize the number of applicants for loans. What is happening today is that, barring very few generalized guidelines, prospective small businessmen are free to apply for financial assistance for any venture they propose to set up. This leads to virtual swamping of the front line units with applications for finance. It is impossible for the managers of the branches to give an even handed consideration to each such proposal. Also, it is difficult for them, by the system of accountability in existence, to reject even one of these. The result is obvious: to delay matters as long as possible and be on the whole indecisive about everything concerning advances. It is an urgent issue, which cries for immediate attention, that some means are found to drastically reduce the number of prospective small business men. In the final analysis, it might be cruel to eliminate and reduce the business community of the nation, but such a revolutionary measure is necessary for the greater good of the nation.

CHAPTER 3

THE SMALL BUSINESSMAN INVESTS HIS LIFE'S DREAM

It is common knowledge that the figure "debt equity ratio" is the keystone for judging the performance of a unit. It measures in one sweep the vital statistics of a unit and reveals symptoms of any malaise afflicting it.

But one should be very careful and wary of using this measuring rod to judge the progress or otherwise of a small business. The debt equity ratio is efficacious as a measure for progress in cases where there is a hiatus between ownership (i.e. supplier of capital) and control (i.e. the executives). A big unit, for whom equity is no problem, has to maintain a healthy ratio with its debts, if only to maintain correct "gearing".

It is well known that the small entrepreneur chronically lacks investible funds and therefore leans heavily on borrowings from financial institutions, especially the nationalized banks. The government is aware of this handicap and yet encourages them to cut a niche for themselves in the country's economy principally because by their proliferations a dent could be made on the unemployment problem facing the country today.

The banks love to consider themselves as financial partners of these small concerns, and yet judge the performance and standing of a small unit by considering its debt equity ratio. This is an exercise in futility, especially in case of small borrowers.

The small industrialists and businessmen who approach banks for assistance make up their lack of investible funds by their sense of total dedication to the cause of their units, which is dearer to them than perhaps their own lives. Their investment in the project consists of their brains and brawns, their past and future and unlike the investment of a portion of one's savings in company shares their stake in the business involves their lifetimes' aspirations; for failure would spell doom for their entire future. For the bank, money lent to a single small unit represents a drop in the ocean of its investment portfolio and it going bad would not tantamount to sleepless nights as in the case of an entrepreneur.

Therefore investment on the part of a small businessman consists of imponderables and intangibles which cannot be converted into black and white figures. If this be the case, considering the figure of debt equity ratio according to accepted definitions would be lopsided and bereft of any real meaning.

Consider the following example:

A firm's statement of affairs as at a particular date reveals the following positions:

	Rs. In thousands
Own Funds	5.0
Borrowed Funds	10.0
	15.0
Fixed Assets	3.0
Current Assets	12.0
	15.0

The turnover for the period was Rs. 15,000.

This unit has landed a continuing order which promises to fetch it a yearly turnover of Rs. 30,000. This is achievable with the existing fixed assets. The rate of profit after taxation is estimated @ 5% on turnover. The blockage in current assets to sustain the increased level of operations is estimated at Rs. 24,000.

The balance-sheet position as at the end of next year (projected) would be as under:

	Rs. in thousands
Own funds	5.0
Profits during the year	1.5
	6.5
Borrowed funds	20.5
	27.0
Fixed Assets	3.0
Current Assets	24.0
	27.0

The above results would indicate deterioration of the debt equity ratio. The question is: should banks lend more funds to support this increase in activities or refrain from doing so because of the proprietor's inability to bring in more capital to improve the debt equity ratio?

Considering the national objective of bolstering the small sector of the economy, it has to be taken for granted that these small people do not have monetary resources to invest in their business. The natural corollary to this is that banks should not give undue importance to the debt equity ratio (since the smallness of equity is an accepted fact) but should lend money on considerations other than the relationship between debt and equity. Such considerations may be the entrepreneur's ability to manufacture additional products or substantial increase in employment opportunities.

Banks should alter their emphasis while taking credit decisions on small units, which have a protected place in our economy, and not follow blindly the text book principles of lending. Decisions on investment in the small sector must bear the stamp of the special considerations that these units are entitled to.

CHAPTER 4

THE ROI SYNDROME

Very often the correct and conservative banker, sitting in judgment over a credit proposal of a small business, would want to work out the return on investment (ROI) ratio and subject it to a comparative study with units selling the same goods or services in big industry.

Such exercises in futility are the result of improper appreciation of the peculiarities inherent in the small sector of the economy. For one, it must be understood that these small businessmen have very little by way of funds to invest in their business. Their investment consists of such intangibles as their brains, brawns and life's dream. The financial institutions are expected, in fact it is a duty cast upon them by the national industrial policy, to provide the small businessman with the required investible funds.

If this simple truth is accepted, a lot of heartburning later is avoided, especially on the ROI issue. Bankers, like all frail humans, would insist upon a fair stake on the part of the entrepreneur, thus leading the entrepreneurs, like all frail mortals to make misrepresentations. This is a vicious circle, which unless broken somehow (possibly by realistic understanding of the situation) leads to untold misery.

Let us examine this ratio of return on investment and try to understand what it denotes as also why it assumes such preponderant role in credit decisions in general.

Simply put, this ratio measures the relationship between the surplus generated and the quantum of investment of the owners of the business.

Purely from the outside, it is a very important indicator of justifiability of the investment, in as much as it is a well-accepted fact in capitalistic form of economy that money should beget money and only those investments are recommended which promise handsome returns. The rate of return, in precise arithmetical terminology, varies from time to time and case to case.

It has to be further remembered that the investor is not entitled to the entire surplus that is generated because from the end result provisions for such items as taxation and appropriations for profit to be retained in the business have to be made. Therefore, to attract a proposed investor to a venture, the expected surplus has to be sufficiently large to absorb the miscellaneous provisions and appropriations.

Therefore ROI measures, in essence, the justifiability of investment in a project and is a potent tool in the hands of credit institutions to judge the viability of the project.

But let us pause for a moment to consider how universal its applicability is, especially in the context of the small sector of the economy. The rate of return (i.e. profitability) is indeed very poor for small business and is a phenomenon which has been dealt with in detail later. It has also been stated earlier that the entrepreneurs' investment in such small ventures is minimal and uncertain.

If these two factors are accepted, if is not difficult to see the fallacy of doing an ROI exercise in case of small units.

The question that needs to be answered is:

If ROI is not the correct tool for judging the "creditability" of small projects, then what is? While a fuller discussion is reserved for a subsequent chapter, it may be worth mentioning a few considerations that should possibly weigh with financial institutions - things like import substitute, export potential, employment creation, etc.

CHAPTER 5

THE PROFITABILITY FACTOR

Very often a small businessman asks "what should be the ideal profitability percentage?" The only answer to this is that there is nothing ideal about this ratio and each case is unique. In a situation when each man faces different kinds of problems, inter-firm comparison is not only hazardous, but would throw up misleading results.

The thing that has to be borne in mind is that the units must run profitably. At what rate the profits accrue does not really matter. All that one has to strive for is that the unit must operate at a level where it is possible to recover all the costs.

The logical question in the face of the aforesaid observation is: why is it not possible to fix a desired profitability ratio in the case of small units? The reasons lie in the uniqueness of the small sector vis-a-vis their big brethren and some of these are listed below:

(1) Most often than not, the small units have hardly any control over the sales price of their products. Because these men are small in every way, they sadly lack the power to dictate terms, to the customer and they often accept orders which yield very little by way of margin.

(2) Because of their smallness, the units in the small sector cannot in most cases tie the customers to any escalation clause. In the face of inflationary conditions the small supplier may find himself with a much reduced margin than what was estimated at the time of placing the orders.

(3) In their anxiety to get orders, the small units often resort to indiscriminate rate cutting. This is because unlike the big sector the small sector in most items does not need manufacturing license. Thus the profitable avenues are soon flooded with a plethora of manufacturing units with the concomitant application of the economic law of supply outstripping demand, thus bringing in its wake all the attendant miseries.

The above three factors would indicate how. difficult it is for the small units to maintain satisfactorily high revenue in the face of these natural limitations. Now for the cost side, the following aspects have to be taken into consideration:

(1) It may not be possible for the small units to economize on costs, since inflation is no respecter of small or big. The same input is dearer over a

period of time and impossible to avoid without impairing efficiency.

(2) Most small units operate for the greater part on borrowed money, whose interest charge is substantial. Interest on borrowed funds is "above the line" adjustment which further erodes into the profitability of a venture. This is unlike the case of a big unit where substantially high own funds are deployed and payment for the use of these funds are "below the line" adjustment in the shape of dividends, which does not affect the profitability as such.

Thus the small units are constantly waging an endless war between fixed revenue and progressively increasing costs. The only way to survive for the small businessman, caught as it were between Scylla and Charybdis, is to gradually increase the scale of operations so that the sheer volume yields a little margin by virtue of unchanging fixed cost.

Therefore, as a matter of rule, to judge whether a small business unit is functioning properly and in the right direction it is essential to watch its turnover over the years, to see that it is steadily increasing thus giving hope that things are perhaps in order. The profit quantum is immaterial. It would indeed suffice if some profits are made, the issue of revenue covering the costs being a predominant factor to judge.

In the light of the above dismal picture of profitability of small scale units, it is indeed a duty cast on them by the peculiar circumstances of these small units never to consciously or unconsciously indulge in diversion of funds. For, any such diversion would cause untold grief. It is also the concomitant duty of the financial institutions to constantly review and recast the repayment obligation, in respect of the term loans as well as applicability of margins so that day to day work is not impaired.

CHAPTER 6

MARGIN MONEY

The most common complaint of bankers and other financial institutions against successful entrepreneurs is that they are unable to provide the minimum margins on their various loan accounts. These institutions are prepared to concede that initially perhaps the technician entrepreneurs are unable to bring in their own stake by way of margin, but it is a common feature that obstinacy creeps in whenever subsequent enhancements are sought for the purpose of doing greater business. On such occasions, inevitably the credit institutions would indicate their willingness to consider the proposal if only matching margins are brought in by these small businessmen.

Such insistence would in all likelihood bring in its trail misrepresentations and outright falsehood on the part of the entrepreneurs.

The whole idea in making the above observation is that is high time for banks and financial institutions to appreciate the position of the small man and therefore relax their margin stipulations. A realistic attitude towards the margin requirements of small units is necessary and unless this is done it is unlikely that small business would flourish in this country.

The keystone of success of a business is in gradually increasing its activities. This calls for higher working capital requirement. Thus banks have to be approached every now and then for higher limits. Even where the volume of production remains stagnant, value wise the same quantum of production would register a rise because of the inflationary factors. This is only to drive home the point that the successful entrepreneur is always in need of higher working capital limits from banks, whether he increases production or allows it to remain constant. Therefore, there appears to be an unending dispute between praying for increased limits and provision of usual margin on the required advances from the banks. In this tussle between higher limits and margin on banks' loan, margin is the sure loser.

The only way margin can be brought in by the small entrepreneur is by ploughing back profits. The irrationality of banks asking for higher margins would be evident from the following example:

A unit which sells Rs. 10 worth of goods per annum enjoys a working capital limit of say Rs. 5 from the bank margin free. At year end the profits earned from the operations is say Re 1, i.e. 10 per cent of the turnover. Assuming that the entire surplus is ploughed back into the business, i.e. no part of this fund has been diverted for acquiring capital assets, an assumption that is idealistic under normal conditions, he is in a position to bring in 20 per cent margin on working capital provided his requirement of finance does not undergo any change.

But as has been mentioned earlier, our entrepreneur may be seeking to increase the sales of his unit two-fold. He may project a turnover of Rs. 20 during the next year, necessitating a working capital requirement of Rs. 10.

Very often the banks would be inclined to give extra assistance to a unit if only it is able to provide the usual margin say 25 per cent. In our example, therefore, on a working capital requirement of Rs. 10, the entrepreneur has to bring in by way of margin Rs. 2.5 when only Re 1 is available. This attitude not only is a deterrent to further growth but is likely to lead a unit into the clutches of sickness and ultimate death. Any constraint on expansion of production is likely to be frustrating to a technician entrepreneur and is a retrograde step for the industrialization and future prosperity of the country as a whole.

Therefore, it is high time for financial institutions and banks to take a realistic stand on the question of margin, so that expansion of activities is not held up for want of the same. It is true that large industries seeking higher limits are guided by the Tandon Committee and Chore Committee recommendations on margins. An exception appears to be in order for the small entrepreneur striving to cut a niche out for himself in the business world. The technician entrepreneur's balance sheet may not reflect a sound financial position in terms of his own stake, yet what is required to be remembered is that unless given an opportunity to expand his activities progressively, he is as good as dead.

CHAPTER 7

QUESTION OF LIQUIDITY

Text books define current ratio as the relationship between current assets and current liabilities. Again, as any text book on financial management would have us believe, this ratio measures the margin of safety of the business as it indicates whether the business has sufficient cushion (i.e. excess of current assets over current liabilities) to pay for the latter if the occasion arises. Furthermore, the same books suggest that, ideally placed, a business organization should have twice the current assets than its current liabilities, which, in other words means that the current ratio should be two. Another concept, the acid test ratio, has been introduced by theoreticians to develop a relationship between those current assets whose liquidity is immediate and the current liabilities.

But all these theoretical formulations have no impact on the small businessman. To the small businessman, perennially short of funds, any suggestion of adhering to the so-called healthy liquidity ratio is simply absurd.

The small businessman operates on a small capital base and since he is not answerable to any one, be can deploy his funds to the best advantage of his concern without fear of being called upon to explain the apparent imbalance in liquidity. He has, by the very nature of his business, to operate on a daily basis and to him the pristine concepts of liquidity, as defined in text books, have no place.

Theoretically, an asset is reckoned to be a current asset if there is a possibility of it being transformed into cash within a year's time. Similarly, a ·liability is current if payment for it has to be made within a year. For obvious reasons, an entrepreneur cannot allow himself the luxury of enjoying such a large time span for important financial decisions. He has to forecast his resource position on a monthly basis, or even on a daily basis.

Consider the following example:

A small businessman wishes to purchase a piece of machinery for Rs. 10. The position of his current assets and current liabilities are as follows:-

Current Liabilities	
Bank borrowings	20
Sundry creditors	15
Provision for taxes	13
	48
Current Assets	
Stocks	14
Bills	30
	44

According to normal judgment, acquisition of fixed assets would further affect the already negative working capital position and hence financial wizards, trained in text book concepts of financial management, are likely to cry a halt to such expenditure which virtually amounts to diversion of working capital funds. The small businessman is undeterred by such restraints. He will, of necessity, have the following considerations in mind:

1. He will first satisfy himself about the liquidity of the current assets and the expected time lag for conversion into cash.

2. He will scrutinize the current liabilities very carefully to see whether payment on them can be delayed or deferred till such time as the current assets are liquefied.

3. He will estimate the additional profitability that the machines will contribute if purchased now, and how soon.

In balance he will take the decision to go in for acquisition of extra fixed assets after weighing all these above factors.

The above exercise only illustrates how these small businessmen, bereft of adequate investible funds, have to take important financial decisions in the face of apparent hazards as revealed by published conventional statements.

The unreliability of published financial statements of small scale industries is being highlighted in a subsequent chapter. Added to this, as would be evident from the above illustration, is the most unorthodox manner in which a small business takes important decisions. This is done primarily by force of circumstances, rather than willful violation of healthy financial norms. It would aid the small borrowers if the financial institutions appreciate the small man's difficulty in adhering to the text book norms and feel the pulse of the unit before shouting from the roof tops that funds have been diverted.

CHAPTER 8

OVERTRADERS BY NATURE

Over trading is a phenomenon frowned upon by any financial management purist. Simply put, it means doing a volume of business which is not warranted by the capital available. The remedy to this situation is to bring in more capital or else curtail the volume of business.

A small businessman's patent diet is overtrading. By the many compulsions he is subjected to, he has no alternative. Text book principles do not hold good in the case of these men as the fear of crash and consequent hazards are a lifelong threat to them. This class of businessmen operates on a very low capital base. Yet they are expected to achieve a turnover of a reasonable amount. In the eternal conflict between low capitalization and need to expand business, the ratios which are indicators of overtrading are the worst sufferers.

Consider the following example. A small businessman's financial position as at the end of the year in which he has achieved a turnover of Rs. 50 is as follows:

Capital	4
Deferred loans	8
Bank borrowings	5
Sundry creditors	3
	20
Fixed Assets	10
Current Assets	10
	20

This business has the potentiality of doubling its turnover during the next year without any addition to its fixed assets. All necessary inputs excepting finance are readily available.

The simple question that anyone should ask in the circumstances is whether the banks should increase the working capital loan based on projected performance or they should deny help to this unit on the ground that it is overtrading as would be evident from the deteriorating debt-equity ratio and poorer current ratio.

What is being suggested is that small units are not capable of adhering to the text book of financial disciple, not by intent to flout ideal standards, but more because given the peculiarities and uniqueness of the small enterprises the standards have to be thrown to the wind. Small industries are indeed very fragile, perpetually suffering from a lack of adequate capital. Yet in order to survive and perform their assigned role in the national economy they have to have a rapidly growing and healthy turnover. Herein lies the genesis of overtrading.

Such being the peculiarity of the small entrepreneur, it is indeed foolish to preach text book slogans of financial discipline to him. One has to be patient and understanding, always ready to stretch out a helping hand as otherwise it will erode the chances ·of survival of the small units, with its concomitant effect on the national economy.

CHAPTER 9

SICKNESS

Sickness of small units defies definition. There have been several attempts by different study groups to evolve a proper definition of the same but none is quite acceptable. The existence of irregularities in the working capital account, or even the gradual shrinkage of the working capital cycle have been cited as possible definitions of sickness. But to the small units, such sophisticated concepts are apt to be of no consequence at all because their needs are so rudimentary.

Perhaps, at least it may be said that the above features appear as symptoms of the dreaded disease of industrial sickness, the causal roots of it have got to be appreciated if a meaningful help to them is proposed.

In the present system, sickness is the inevitable fate of every small unit. The small businessmen are basically frail creatures who are likely to buckle under the slightest adversity because of their limited resources. The small units are prone to this malady more than their larger brethren because of their inability to withstand the slightest pressure. And in an uncertain business environment, smooth running is all but an alien concept.

It has got to be appreciated that sickness creeps in not only because of capital shortage, but may be attributed to a thousand and one "non-monetary" causes. In the course of the active life of a business enterprise, it has to contend with the interplay of market forces and not being strong or sturdily built very often the free economy forces take the upper hand. And the small units, unable to grapple with this pressure, ultimately fall hapless victims to this unpredictable phenomenon.

Another reason as to why small units are extra prone to sickness is the tremendous commercial ignorance of the entrepreneurs. Whereas their technical knowledge is without peer, the same thing cannot be said about their business acumen. They would so regulate their affairs that their units would ultimately become not a viable one.

Time over again it has been stressed by the pundits that industrial sickness is inevitable if technological changes are not made with the times and if production processes languish behind in improvement and updating. For the small man, with limited resources at his command and professionalization of management strikingly absent, adherence to the latest technology is indeed futile to expect. And small business, being basically one man shows, the technical expertise is confined usually to the proprietor himself. It is physically and humanly impossible for a single man, harried as he is, to keep tab of the swiftly changing technical scene.

It is because of the peculiarities of small business in this country, i.e. too much reliance on the abilities of a single man to steer a business venture to success that the imbibing of the latest technological innovation suffers. Not only that, in the case of enterprises just set up, technology may have been given a second seat because of capital constraints and availability of cheap substitute labour.

It is indeed, praiseworthy for the entrepreneur that such alternative manner, in the circumstances unavoidable, has to be made. However such enterprises suffer in the long run because of inability to adapt themselves to the changing technological scenario.

In a highly competitive world, charged as it is with intense business compulsions, not only process diversification (keeping pace with technological progress) but also product diversification has to be resorted to, if only to survive. Small business suffers because of inflexibility and imperviousness to change which again can be traced to shortage of resources and over-dependence on the abilities of a single man. Strategic planning, a concept and exercise inescapable for modern day survival, is painfully absent in the small business sector. It is their custom, dictated by their handicaps, to stick to the initial technology and product range chosen, for any deviation therefrom would involve spending a lot of money which they can ill afford and as well as lead to a radical alteration in the proprietor-technologist axis.

CHAPTER 10

REHABILITATION

It is indeed extremely difficult to rehabilitate small units principally because the environment under which they have to function remains unchanged and there is no radical departure from the reasons which led to the initial malady. It is matter of shame, with the consequence of huge monetary loss for the financial institutions, that even after pumping a huge amount of money, in the final analysis these have to be written off as bad debt.

Why is this so? It is high time that we take stock of the entire pattern of help to the small sector of the economy and try to underscore the basic defects.

It is not the quantum of finance that would cure the sickness but the government's sincerity in smoothening the rough roads of a business venture. And it is the duty of the government to see to it that small units are not wanting in the basic inputs at any time.

Rehabilitation programmes do not prove successful in respect of small units because there is little assurance over the supply of the three basic inputs - men, money and materials. There appears to be nothing SPECIAL in respect of rehabilitating small units and they are subjected to the same uncertain market forces and they are expected to survive the vicissitudes in the same way as the healthy ones. It is indeed a myth to expect that a unit which is sick and is in receipt of rehabilitation finance would be resilient enough to conquer the uncertainties and enigmas of a modern day business stress situation and emerge successful. What is therefore needed is a crutch or walking stick to help these units along the way. And this extra help must be a deliberate effort on the part of the government.

Therefore extra financial borrowing limits sanctioned in favour of sick small units is not going to cure sickness unless conscious efforts are made to view indulgently the small units' requirements of men, money, materials and market. It is worth appreciating that merely giving them a fresh lease of life would only prolong the agony as unable to withstand the business world by themselves, death/decay are a sure fate awaiting them - the only difference being that a greater amount of public money is thus wasted in the process.

Rehabilitation finance, if it has to be effective and meaningful, has to be a total package of help and assistance to the small sector. Piecemeal help would surely lead to nowhere and is doomed from the start, as is happening in the present day instances. This perhaps would unravel the mystery as to why, rehabilitation finance poured so generously on sick small units are a failure in the long run. And unless effective help from the government or its agencies is assured in respect of the four M's, rehabilitation effort should not be undertaken by any financial institution as money is only one of the basic inputs necessary to succeed in business ventures.

Therefore apart from financial assistance, which cannot be underplayed, help in the form of timely, easy and cheap availability of various other inputs have got to be arranged. Whereas small units have to be looked upon with special favour, more so is expected in case of sick units in receipt of rehabilitation assistance. And unless this is done consciously by the government of the day, rehabilitation programme might as well be written off.

If deserving sick units have to be rehabilitated, sometimes it would be necessary for the financial institutions to forgo a part of their previous outstanding. This is because the principal and the consequent interest thereon prove a drag on the units thus preventing rehabilitation. If the financial institutions are prepared to forgo only a portion of their dues, it would indeed save huge amounts from being turned into bad debt. Obstinate insistence by the financial institutions to recover the entire dues leads to drawing up of over-ambitious rehabilitation programme and has thus proven to be the bane of rehabilitation financing. If some method could be found where, in deserving cases, a portion of the outstanding could be written off, this programme could be more effective. Then again to do so it is necessary to revolutionize the entire concept of assistance to the small man.

CHAPTER 11

SECURITY-BASED VS ACTIVITY-BASED LENDING

Security consciousness has so permeated the thinking of bankers in general that they are unable to dissociate themselves from the lasso when considering the financial needs of a small business man. This particular quirk in the bankers of this country is, to say the least, inimical to the growth prospects of this sector and would hardly help the small business man to ultimately survive. Another expression of the security based approach is in the way the borrowing limits are calculated. These are inevitably based on the highest level of blockages of funds in stocks and receivables and do not usually take into account the usual seasonal/periodic fluctuations. This method of reckoning has two major flaws:

1. Whenever the requirements are lesser than the prescribed limit, the borrowers are tempted to withdraw the surplus funds in their accounts which they can easily do so because of absence of monitoring by the bankers.

2. In times of actual need being in excess of the borrowing limits, the small business men find it extremely difficult to convince their bankers about the genuine needs since the bankers are reluctant to deviate from the preset path.

The only way out of this apparent difficulty is to require units to submit weekly/fortnightly cash budget and after usual scrutiny fix the borrowing limit accordingly. The activity based lending so proposed would be beneficial for both the borrowers and banks as it would inter-alia help in the following:

1. The drawing up of cash budget would regulate withdrawals from account and would hopefully prevent borrowers from withdrawing more funds than are actually necessary.

2. Unavoidable delay in receiving payment, the usual bane of small borrowers, is automatically taken care of in the cash budget system. The borrowers have to convince their bankers the reason for deviation from cash budget, if any, submitted by them. This leads to a constant dialogue with the banker, first at the time of consideration of the cash budget as well as at the time of requesting/ considering deviations. This interaction between, the banker and small businessmen is indeed a desirable feature as thereby the former would be able to appreciate the needs and peculiarities of the latter.

3. If borrowing limits are fixed on the basis of budgets it is only to be hoped that decision to exceed the limits (in the security based approach)

would not be as tardy as before. Quick and instant decisions are the keystone of success of the small businessmen and working under the constraints of fixation of borrowing limits prove counter to quick decisions. Requests for additional drawings, however genuine they were, would be lost in bureaucratic tangle, with the consequent delay and inaction.

The insistence of margin by the bankers would be better served if cash budget system were followed. The margin or the borrowers' portion of the investment is now adhered to more in the breach and it would be helpful for the bankers to monitor the results of cash budget, wherefrom it would be evident whether the borrowers have the required stake in the business.

Moreover the financial institutions must lessen their reliance on the borrowing firms' financial statements. Rarely does the Profit & Loss Account and the Balance

Sheet of a small firm tend to reflect its true picture. It is only realistic to appreciate that these statements are drawn up with the bankers or the income tax department in mind. This is done principally to justify to the financial institutions the need for so much bank credit - which otherwise would not be forthcoming, and to evade paying back to the government in the form of taxation on its profit a substantial amount of money earned by it. The small units, unlike their big counterparts can afford to tamper with the bottom line results because (1) the small man's accounts are not subject to the same strict audit vigilance as are those of the larger units and (2) the small man combines in himself the role of the owner as well as the Chief Executive. By virtue of being the owner of the business, he is accountable to none for its results. He is the veritable master of all he surveys and he does not have irate and temperamental shareholders to please and satisfy.

All the above factors contribute to the financial statement revealing a distorted picture of the firm's state of affairs - and to place Bible-like reliance on these figures would indeed be a foolhardy mistake on the part of the financial institutions - but tragically that is exactly what is happening in the context of security based assessment of financial needs of the small borrowers. Calculations are bound to go awry if in the first place the basic premise is wrong. And the financial institutions would only find themselves in a notionally happy position having their paper work all right - but fully knowing the uselessness of this exercise as the figures on the basis of which the limits have been worked out do not conform to reality.

Cash budget procedure of appraisal would help in eliminating this underlying risk of reliance on doubtful figures. Cash budget would help to realistically assess and meet the fund requirement of small units.

CHAPTER 12

EFFECTIVE HELP FOR SMALL UNITS PROPOSED

Small is beautiful. This remark of Schumacher has, however, thorny connotations as the proverbial rose as far as small industries in this country are concerned. Be that as it may, the government has chosen to encourage the small sector, perhaps as a panacea for the problem-ridden economy.

Pursuant to this declaration, the industrial policy of this country has been framed to give a fillip to this sector. The government has given incentives to the small sector to help them counter the overriding advantage of their big brethren.

But all these measures do not really help small industries. While the intentions are good, what mars the otherwise beatific scene is the total lack of dedication among the persons charged with the execution of the same.

This apart, the very conception of help to the small sector is misleading and lacking in the correct emphasis. Help, to be more meaningful, should be of a continuing nature, and not a mere enticement to jump into the fray. Sadly, that is exactly what the package of assistance to the small sector denotes today.

There is no dearth of enthusiasm on the part of state government agencies or financial bodies to promote the small scale sector. Attractive incentives are given for starting small ventures. There have been instances when banks have finalized credit proposals in the course of joint seminars.

Once started, these small enterprises are left on their own to fend for themselves, often with disastrous consequences.

It is of fundamental importance to remember who and what the small businessmen are made of. Basically they are technician entrepreneurs, first generation businessman with very little or no monetary resources of their own. The only assets they possess are technical skill and an unbounded enthusiasm to conquer all obstacles. There is no denying the fact that in the initial stages, the entrepreneur's honesty of purpose is supreme, for any later infraction we have to blame the circumstances only.

What then are these circumstances and to what extent are the various institutions involved responsible?

After being launched into a business venture with the package of incentives used as a carrot, the entrepreneur seems to be a neglected child. No state agency, no financial institution (contrary to publicity) comes forward to lend a helping hand in times of distress. All worries, all problems (be it non-availability of quota material, or the lack of adequate finance, or even the government's refusal to agree to an escalation clause) belong only to the hapless entrepreneur, and since nothing succeeds like success, he is heralded as a successful entrepreneur if he can solve his problems on his own.

It has to be remembered that the small industrialist is a person whose shock-absorbing capacity is zero. This is primarily because he has hardly any built in resources to fall back on for the rainy day or credits of reasonable amounts from the market.

That being briefly the general profile of the small industrialist, serious attention must be given by the planners as to whether small is really beautiful and if so, how these small units can be helped meaningfully, instead of just giving them a slogan lacking in material content.

A small unit has to be helped and aided for a long time and such assistance has to be a continuous affair. It does not serve the national objective if small units are encouraged only at their inception, and left to brave the vicissitudes thereafter.

The government must realize this in-born difficulty in the small sector and must come up with a realistic plan of action whereby these troubles can be obviated.

The government should take care of the following:

a) Smooth availability of inputs: It has to be ensured that the small industrialists do not face at any time paucity of correct inputs - be it materials, finance, power, etc. Failure to get the right amount of inputs would jeopardize the very existence of small industries because, as has been mentioned earlier, these small units lack the resilience to withstand the least amount of disruption.

b) There should be a tribunal type of body which should look into the entrepreneur's grievances. Such a tribunal should be empowered to take effective steps, and quickly, to ameliorate their genuine difficulties.

To this commission the small entrepreneur must have free access. This commission should not only act as a watch-dog but also would be available for giving counsel and advice to the small men. Instances such as that of unfair activities indulged in by persons in authority could be brought to the notice of the commission who would investigate these promptly and recommend suitable punishment. It is hoped that by this measure the oppression sought to be perpetrated on these small men by people who can make or undo the prospects of a small industry would be removed. Also, this commission may judge the sudden requirements of finance of these small units and recommend suitable bank credits. In one word this commission would be entrusted to look into the welfare of small scale industries in general and the weaker section in particular.

c) Since modern business operates in a highly specialized environment, the success of a present day venture is partially dependent upon the extent of specialized expertise the small unit is able to draw upon.

CHAPTER 13

CHANGE OF HEART

It has to be emphasized that unless a change of heart is brought to bear on the small industries by everyone concerned, survival itself would become difficult. One has to clearly understand that small industry is the sick child of the nation, and if one is interested to see it alive, it has got to be pampered and generous handicaps extended to it.

Such a liberal attitude is difficult to expect from every human, and because of the imperviousness to appreciate the difficulties of the small men, that forms the main bane of assistance to this sector.

Let us try to examine the areas where such co-operation is necessary but is lacking. The small industries are businessmen by courtesy only - and they cannot make a success of their ventures without active help and concession from outsiders. This class of industry is being actively encouraged by the government as it tends to make an impact on the huge unemployment problem on a relatively small investment. But such good intentions are likely to vanish into thin air if the basic vulnerability of the small is not admitted and appreciated by the powers that be. It is not possible for the small to grapple with the uncertain business environment in the same manner and with the same amount of resilience as their big brethren. And unless this basic fact about small industry is understood, encouragement for growth of this sector will surely lead to the inevitable disaster of sickness, closure and national wastage.

The small industries need constant counseling and supervision right from the day the project is conceived;

and if the government of the day is unable to provide this extra crutch to the small men, it should not, in all fairness, mouth pious sentiments of encouraging this sector. What actually is happening today to the small sector is that the government is encouraging units to be set up in this sector (and liberal promotional aids are taken resort to) and once set up, they are left to combat with the business vicissitudes by themselves - and outside governmental assistance sadly lacking either because of ignorance of the small man's needs or because of lack of properly motivated personnel to provide succor to the small industries.

Without this conscious help to the small men, survival is well-nigh impossible, and an institutional mechanism has to be devised to assist this sector - for, as is often the case, the small men do not know when to turn to experts for counseling for the simple reason that their reflexes are not in tune with the modern day business culture.

When such is the case, monitoring of small units on a day-to-day basis should be entrusted to an outside body. Care should however be taken that this measure in no way impinges upon or appears to impinge upon the freedom of the small man. Because the small man values the concept of freedom more than ever in starting a venture of his own.

For the reality of the situation is that the entrepreneurs possess king size egos which have to be countered in the most subtle manner if a success is to be made of their ventures. The entrepreneurs are likely to resist any interference in their affairs, however well-meaning they might be. They tend to overplay the concept of freedom and any compulsion to have their affairs scrutinized by an outside body is bound to arouse suspicion. Therefore the whole arrangement of providing expert help to the entrepreneur has to be dealt with caution and circumspection. Yet it is undeniably true that a small unit cannot do without outside expert assistance, for the simple reason the entrepreneur cannot himself be a master of all facets of knowledge required to run a business. Therefore the situation of helping the small business in this country is fraught with great many imponderables - and the success of these ventures cannot be ensured unless there is an all-round change of heart.

CHAPTER 14

EPILOGUE

In this book I have tried to point out some of the genuine difficulties of the small business men and have sought to suggest some remedial measures to alleviate their lot. If the government of the day cannot take positive steps to defend and protect the hapless bunch of small businessmen in the areas suggested hereinbefore, then I sincerely believe that it would be better for everyone to do away with the active promotion of the small sector.

One of the promotional devices used by the government is the reservation of more than eight hundred industries which are beyond the pale of medium and large scale industries and are strictly reserved for the small scale sector. While admitting the intention being above suspicion, what is happening in the long run is that in the face of the numerous constraints of small industries in general, quality of production takes a back seat which ultimately affects the customers.

It is my submission, therefore, that if the government is not in a position to render meaningful help to the small men to overcome their inherent difficulties, such a system of reservation of production areas must be stopped in the larger interest of consumers and free inter-play of market forces (be it small or large) be given full sway.

Scrapping the promotion of the small would mean directing the financial institutions accordingly. This however does not mean stopping of the favourable interest rates or looking upon the small men with an indulgent eye. In India, owing to its peculiarities of distribution of wealth, such benevolent measures must continue. What is being suggested is that the larger units be allowed unfettered competition with the small in an effort to enhance the quality of the final product. The justification of the small men will then lie not upon protectionist policy of the government, but upon how effectively it can compete with their big brethren.

This policy, if adopted by the government, would result in a severe curtailment of applicants desirous of setting up industries and will encourage only those who can stand on their own legs and effectively call the tune. As has been mentioned earlier concessional financing should continue to be made available to deserving entrepreneurs - the final decision to do so should remain in the hands of the financial institutions, which shorn of pressing national duties would, I believe, be better equipped to look upon the issue in a better perspective than most others.

APPENDIX: PRESENT GOVERNMENT POLICY

The following is an extract from Guidelines for Industries published by the Ministry of Industry, Govt. of India, relating to the Small Scale Industries: -

COMPREHENSIVE ASSISTANCE PROGRAMME

The Small Industries Development Organisation (SIDO) of the Department Industrial Development has a network of 25 Small Industries Service Institutes, 20 Branch Institutes, 41 Extension Centres, 4 Regional Testing Centres, 2 Tool Rooms and Training Centres, 2 Training centres, 5 Production Centres and 1 Product and Process Development Centre throughout the country.

The assistance programme of the SIDO includes supply of information on prospects of items which could be taken up in the small scale sector; provision of economic, technical and managerial services, drawing up of schemes and industry prospect sheets; common facility and extension services: training in management and technical trades; assistance in modernisation and technological developments and guidance in the procurement of machinery, factory sites, finance, marketing, participation in Government stores purchase, etc. Besides, the State Governments, through their respective Directorates of Industries and other States agencies, assist small entrepreneurs through allotment of land/factory sheds, supply of scarce categories of raw materials including imported ones and provide financial assistance, both for long and short term requirements.

RESERVATION OF INDUSTRIES/ITEMS

Reservation of selected industries/items for exclusive development in the small scale sector is one of the measures adopted for accelerating the growth of this sector by providing a field where small entrepreneurs need not face any adverse competition from the large scale sector. The Government of India has so far reserved over 800 items for exclusive manufacture in the small scale sector.

REGISTRATION AND PRODUCTION RETURN

In the small scale sector, a prospective entrepreneur need not obtain any licence for setting up a unit provided the item of manufacture is not governed by special regulation. However, entrepreneurs in their own interest are advised to register their own units with the Directorate of Industries of the States where their units are located irrespective of whether or not they require any assistance from the Government. Registration helps a unit to obtain all facilities and assistance from Government under the programmes of development of small scale industries as announced from time to time.

MONTHLY PRODUCTION RETURN

All small scale units are required to submit monthly production returns showing the raw materials consumed, production, employment, etc. to the Directorate of Industries and the Small Industries Service Institute in the State, Development Commissioner, Small Scale Industries, New Delhi. Failure to submit such returns within the prescribed limit may constitute adequate grounds for refusing to sponsor application for import assistance/allocation of raw materials and ultimately might lead to the deregistration of the unit. The data received from the small scale industrial units through these production returns will on one hand enable the State Industries Deptt/Office of the DC(SSI), Government of India to maintain an up-to-date picture regarding production and growth of small scales sector and will facilitate the Government in arriving at realistic estimates of the requirement of the small scale sector in respect of scarce raw material, finance and other essential inputs on the other. Thus, regular submission of these returns by the small scale industrial units will serve their own larger interest.

TECHNICAL ASSISTANCE

As soon as the entrepreneur has decided about the line of manufacture, he can seek the help of the local SISI or any other promotional agencies for preparing a detailed scheme for setting up his unit. The SIDO has already prepared a large number of schemes/reports and other literature containing technical and general information on a wide range of industries/items. The SISIs and Extension Centres provide technical assistance and advice in the day-to-day working of the unit. While visiting the units, the technical officers also provide suitable on-the-spot assistance.

TRAINING

The training programme organised by the various SISIs and their Extension Centres aim at improving the technical skills of the workers and acquainting the entrepreneurs with advanced production and management techniques. For specialised courses, 3 Prototype Production-cum-Training centres have been set up at Okhla (New Delhi), Rajkot (Gujarat) and Howrah (West Bengal) under the National Small Industries Corporation. An Institute for Advanced Training in Tool Making has been established at Hyderabad and another for Electrical Measuring Instruments at Bombay. Small industries are encouraged to avail themselves of the facilities of these institutes through payment or stipends to the trainees. Besides, two Tool Rooms and Training Centres have been set up at Calcutta and Ludhiana for providing training in tools, jigs and fixtures, etc. The State Governments have also set up a number of training centres.

The following government and institutional agencies are providing different types of financial assistance to small industries:

Risk Capital:

- State Financial Corporation.
- Small Industries Corporation.

Long-term and Medium-term Loans:

- State Directorate of Industries (under the State Aid to Industries Act.)
- State Financial Corporation.
- Commercial Banks.

Short-term/Working Capital:

- Commercial Banks.

Hire-Purchase Scheme:

- National Small Industries Corporation.

- Small Industries Development Corporation.

RISK CAPITAL

The State Financial Corporation provides seed capital assistance to entrepreneurs, particularly to new technician entrepreneurs and entrepreneurs taking up projects in backward areas. The assistance, which is provided under a scheme formulated by the Industrial Development Bank of India is in the form of equity or soft loan towards meeting the gap between the normal expected level of promoters' contribution as envisaged by the SFC and the actual amount that the promoter could bring on his own subject to a ceiling of 20 per cent of the project cost or Rs 23 lakhs whichever is lower. All types of industrial concerns proprietory, partnership and private as also public limited companies are eligible for assistance under the scheme. The IDBI also has another scheme operated through the agency of SIDO/SIICs covering entrepreneurs establishing projects up to a cost of Rs. 1 crore.

Several State Small Industries Development Corporation participate in equity capital.

SEED/MARGIN MONEY SCHEME

Seed/Margin Money Assistance would be provided as loan component under DIC programme to enable the State Governments and Union Territory Administrations for promotion of small industries in semi-urban and rural areas. The funds could be utilised for margin money assistance upto 10 per cent of the total fixed capital investment of small units with investment on plant and machinery not exceeding Rs. 1 lakh; seed money to State Corporations to small units; and assistances for consultancy services to small units. The area covered under the scheme would be towns and villages having a population of less than 50,000. For entrepreneurs belonging to Scheduled Castes and Scheduled Tribes, seed money assistance may be 15 per cent of the total fixed capital investment or Rs. 20,000 whichever is lower.

STATE AID TO INDUSTRIES ACT

Under the State Aid to Industries Act, State Government provide finance in the form of loans, guarantees for loans raised from banks, subscription to shares and debentures etc. In most of the States, loans upto Rs. 1,000/- are advanced on personal bonds, upto Rs. 5,000/- against one or more personal security and above Rs. 5,000/- at 75 per cent of the value of security offered (land, buildings, machinery, equipment, stocks and their assets including those created out of the loans). These loans are advanced on soft terms and are repayable in easy instalments spread over 10 years. The rates of interest vary from State to State. Some State Governments offer rebates for prompt repayment.

State Financial Corporations have been established in all the States with the object of providing medium and long term finance to small scale industries out of their own funds besides disbursing loans as agents of the State Governments. In the case of limited companies and cooperative societies, loans are advanced from Rs. 10,000/- to Rs. 30 lakhs and in the case of others upto Rs. 15 lakhs. The Corporations generally maintain a margin varying from 25% to 50%. The rate of interest charged by the Financial Corporations varies from State to State. Most of the Corporations also allow a rebate for prompt repayment.

COMMERCIAL BANK

Credit facilities at concessional rates are extended to small industries against the security of raw materials and/or finished or semi-finished goods under lock and key or factory type basis by all scheduled commercial banks. Most of the banks have a slab rate system, with lower interest rates by smaller advances.

Composite loans are now being sanctioned by the banks and the Reserve Bank of India has issued instructions to all the commercial banks in 1979 to dispose of the loan applications expeditiously.

RAW MATERIAL

(i)   Imported

The small scale units are entitled to import of raw materials according to the Import Trade Control Policy as announced every year. The import policy was reviewed and the procedure was simplified during 1979. The import policy was further liberalised in 1979-80 and made them very much beneficial to the small scale sector.

For getting imported raw materials the units are required to apply in the prescribed form to the Director of Industries, who in turn recommends their cases to the Joint Chief Controller of Imports & Exports of the region concerned for the issue of import licences/release orders.

In case of new small scale units, import licences upto Rs. 3,00,000/- in value are issued on the recommendation of the sponsoring authorities. For additional requirements of raw materials the actual users could seek supplementary licence through the sponsoring authorities.

Special facilities are offered for new or proposed units set up in backward areas or by graduates/diploma holders in professional subjects or by ex-service-men/persons belonging to weaker section of the society.

Import licences for raw materials and consumable spares to small scale units including cottage industries are issued for imports against free foreign exchange.

(ii)   Indigenous

Most of the raw materials produced indigenously have been decontrolled and units are free to take these materials directly from the producers, stockyards of the producers, State Small Industries Corporations and from the open market. However, wherever there is some control, the unit has to apply to the State Director of Industries, who will allocate the material to the unit.

In case of certain scarce raw materials, efforts are afoot to assess the capacity of each of the small industrial units and ensure supply of such indigenous and imported raw materials on the basis of their capacities. Since it is not possible for small industrialists to buy certain types of scarce raw materials in large quantities, the State Small Industries Corporation obtain them in bulk and supply to individual entrepreneurs.

In order to ensure quick and efficient delivery they have opened raw material depots at suitable centres. Besides, action is being taken to create buffer stocks of materials for meeting the emergency requirements.

INDUSTRIAL ESTATES

Industrial Estates with pre-built factory sheds/developed plot have been set up in different parts of the country for coordinated, intensified and integrated development of small scale industries. Besides, developed sites have also been provided to small entrepreneurs to erect their own factory building. These industrial estates/developed plots have been located at suitable sites after proper techno-economic surveys in developed areas as well as at promising growth centres in rural and backward areas. The industrial estates provide at one place all the requisite facilities necessary for starting small scale industries viz, water, electricity, transport, banks, post-offices, canteens, watch and ward, first-aid, etc. and hence help small industrialists save their time and resources on obtaining these facilities by themselves. Besides, industrial estates bring a number of different industrial units together and facilitate establishment of common facility servicing centres, introduction of modern techniques, collective purchase of raw materials and sale of finished goods.

The State Governments provide a number of facilities to the small entrepreneurs in the industrial estates. These include subsidy on rent for factory accommodation, allotment of sheds on hire-purchase basis as well as outright sale of sheds, reasonable charges for water and electricity, exemption from sales tax on certain categories of industries for a given period of time, loans to small industries in non-conforming areas for shifting to industrial estates/developed sites, etc.

With a view to supplementing Government efforts at providing work sites to the small entrepreneurs in the industrial estates set up by the state Governments/State Corporations it has been the policy of the Government to increasingly encourage small entrepreneurs to form cooperative societies/joint stock companies to set up their own industrial estates on cooperative lines.

Details regarding the availability of sheds/developed plots in the industrial estates/developed sites set up by the State Governments/State Corporations and the scheme for setting up cooperative industrial estates may be obtained by the small industrialists/entrepreneurs from the concerned State Directorate of Industries/Corporation.

MARKETING

The National Small Industries Corporation helps small industries to participate in the Government sale-purchase programme. Till November, 1980, 382 items have been reserved by the Director General Supplies and Disposals for exclusive purchase from the small scale sector. In addition, graded reservation of items for purchases upto 75 per cent and 50 percent of the requirements have been introduced this year and 11 and 15 items respectively have been specified under these categories. A price preference of upto 15 per cent is given to small scale units in respect of items which are purchased both from large scale and small scale sectors. Besides, the State Governments have also their store-purchase programme. Information in this regard may be obtained from the SISI's and the Directors of Industries.

In order to help small entrepreneurs in marketing their goods, the Government of India sanctioned setting up of 9 Trade Centres in various parts of the country. The centres serve as meeting points for buyers and the sellers and provide services such as permanent exhibitions of small industry products; industrial information; library and documentation; testing and quality control, etc. The Centres are located at Jaipur, Bangalore, Kanpur, Ludhiana, Hyderabad, Ahmedabad, Chandigarh, Bhubaneswar and Cochin. The scheme has since been transferred to State Government.

SUB-CONTRACTING EXCHANGE

With a view to providing effective support to small scale units in securing ancillary jobs from large and medium undertakings in the country, SIDO has established 16 sub-contracting exchanges in Small Industries Service Institutes. These exchanges on an average assist more than 5000 small scale units per annum.

NUCLEUS PLANTS

Nucleus plants are proposed to be set up in selected districts for achieving rapid industrial growth by developing ancillary industries. Nucleus plants would concentrate on assembling the products of the ancillary units falling within its orbit, or producing the inputs needed by a large number of smaller units and making adequate marketing arrangements. The nuclei will also ensure a widely spread pattern of investment and employment and will distribute the benefits of industrialisation to the maximum possible extent. The nucleus plants would also work for upgrading the technology of small units. Small is beautiful only if it is growing just as the phased manufacturing programme with a view to reducing reliance on imported components and materials played an important role in diversifying our industrial structure, a carefully worked out time bound programme for greater ancillarisation in certain industries will contribute considerably towards dispersal of industry and growth of entrepreneurship.

MODERNISATION

The programme of modernisation aims at identifying the problems of productivity efficiency and obsolescence in small scale units and to keep them abreast with the latest information on production processes, product designs, technological development and training facilities through provision of an effective technical consultancy service and other forms of assistance. As a part of the programme, modernisation courses, industrial workshops, industrial clinics, seminars, inplant studies, etc. are being organised on a continuing basis to guide and motivate the small scale units to adopt modern production and management concepts and to improve their competitive strength. Professional consultants are also employed for this purpose.

DISTRICT INDUSTRIES CENTRES

The District Industries Centres (DICs) programme was launched on 1st May, 1978 with a view to provide an integrated administrative framework at the district level to look after the problems of industrialization in the district in a composite manner.

By the end of March 1980, 382 DICs covering 392 districts out of a total of 406 districts in the country were sanctioned. The scheme is now under review and a more effective alternative for effecting co-ordinated and sustained growth of industries in the country will be evolved soon.

TESTING CENTRES

Four Regional Testing Centres have been set up at New Delhi, Calcutta, Bombay and Madras for providing testing facilities and assistance to the small scale units in improving the quality of their products and enabling the small units to produce goods conforming to Indian Standards Institution specifications. These facilities relate to testing in the field of engineering metallurgical, chemical and electrical trades.

FIELD TESTING STATIONS

The need for having a chain of testing centres with specialised product orientation at places having local concentration of industries is now felt. These Field Testing Stations would provide facilities for testing of the main performance specifications, so that the manufacturers could then take it to the Regional Testing Centres or other National Test House Centres to get full-fledged test certificates.

PROCESS-CUM-PRODUCT DEVELOPMENT CENTRES

A Process-cum-Product Development Centre has been set up at Ranchi for effecting transfer of technology in glass and ceramics industries. It is proposed to establish a network of such centres for different product groups during 1980-85. These centres will be located in the respective SISI's itself.

CENTRAL TOOL ROOMS AND TRAINING CENTRES

Two Central Tool Rooms and Training Centres are at present under operation/establishment at Calcutta and Ludhiana with the assistance of Government of Denmark and Federal Republic of Germany respectively. The Tool Room at Calcutta has already started functioning. The Tool Room at Ludhiana is in the process of being set up. These projects will provide training in the fields of tool designs and manufacture and common facilities for production of special purpose jigs, fixtures, press tools, dies, moulds and other tools. Similar facilities are available at the Tool Rooms in Delhi and Bangalore, which are under the State control.

A Hand Tool Institute is being set up at Jullundur. This Institute will cater to the research, design and development needs of the small scale hand tools industry in the country.

CENTRAL INSTITUTE OF TOOL DESIGN

The Central Institute of Tool Design has been set up in Hyderabad with the assistance of United Nations Development Programme and International. Labour Organisations. The main objectives of the Institute are:

1. Training of technical personnel preferably of small scale industries in the design and manufacture of tools, jigs, fixtures, dies and moulds;

2. Provision of advisory, consultancy and common service facilities to small scale industries including assistance in the design and development of tools for various processes;

3. Production on a limited basis of tools, jigs, fixtures, gauges, dies and moulds etc. and

4. Recommending measures to standardise components of tools, jigs, fixtures, dies and moulds.

SMALL INDUSTRIES EXTENSION TRAINING INSTITIUTE, HYDERABAD

The SIET Institute has been set up in Hyderabad by the Government of India to provide training, research and consultancy services to small industry. It provides comprehensive training in industrial management covering all aspects of industrial development such as materials management, production management, information storage & retrieval, documentation system, market survey and demand analysis, feasibility survey and analysis etc. It has now become an institution of national importance in the field of industrial management training and research. Its client organisations include financial institutions, commercial banks, State and National Level Financial Corporations, Small Industry Development Organisation, Academic and Research Institutions and small entrepreneurs.

INSTITUTE FOR DESIGN OF ELECTRICAL MEASURING INSTRUMENTS

The Institute for Design of Electrical Measuring Instruments (IDEMI), Bombay offers various services to suit the needs of the instrument industry. The services offered in general are Technical Consultancy, Instrument Design, Prototype Fabrication, Laboratory Facilities, Tool Making and Tool Design Facilities and Training in the instruments field. These services are generally offered to small scale industries.

ACKNOWLEDGEMENTS

It is not possible to end this book without acknowledging the contributions of some of the people who were responsible for bringing the publication of this book into fruition.

My mother, the late Krishna Chaudhuri has been the driving force in my life apart from being my father's soulmate and biggest source of strength. Her meticulous record-keeping resulted in the safe preservation of this manuscript so that it could be found and published even after 22 years of my father's (the author's) demise,

My wife Kamalika Chaudhuri has been instrumental in getting this book published. It was primarily her idea to get the manuscript published and insisted we find a good publisher for the same. It was with her support and encouragement that I was able to do the necessary spadework to get this project off the ground.

And last but not the least my daughter Nayantrika whose keen interest in her late grandparents along with her never-ending questions often forced me to think back deeply into the past and reach back into a few forgotten memories.

------ Ayan Chaudhuri